Creating a Path ...
... Leaving a Trail

To Vicky

Love

Karen

xx

Rising Sun, my Indian Spirit Guide

Creating a Path ...
... Leaving a Trail

Confessions of a Medium (Part 1)
Learning from loss, love and life

Karen Teague

Quicksilver Publications

First published by Quicksilver Publications in the United
Kingdom in 2015.

ISBN - 978-0-9932872-2-0

Type set in Comic Sans 12 / 18 pt.
Origination by Patricia J Mills
Printed by Grosvenor Group (Print Services) Ltd, EC2A 3HB

Dedication

In memory of

VERA WENDY BURLING
13th February 1934 to 6th September 2003

Thank You.

My Mother
My All, My Everything.
I Love and Adore You Always.

Karen.

Contents

Acknowledgements

To my Dad, Charles Burling. The strongest, kindest, most supportive man I know. I love you, Dad.

My love, thanks and pride go out to my children, Emma and Adam, who never ever gave up on me. I love you unconditionally.

To my grandchildren, Alfie, Louie, Freddie and Evelyn. To my family, and brothers Ross and Nigel for having to deal with this crazy different woman, Karen. Thank you for your love. To their wives for making them happy.

To my friends – I love you and thank you for your never ending support.

To Lorraine and Terry for typing and correcting my mistakes with love, and to my publisher Trish for being so patient.

Preface

The world between the 'what was' and 'what is', that world I live in, offers a feeling of peace and security to me. At times I feel I am crossing a bridge of magnificence. I cannot expect anyone to understand my world unless they see it themselves. I am driven by desire to change the beliefs, thoughts and feelings of all of humanity. To live with a purpose, justice and a time of peace and love.

My name does not mean much to most people. Karen. Nothing spectacular, but the chosen name of my parents. I cannot pretend to understand myself, and at times in my life I have felt pure torment within. You see, I flit from one life to the next. Living in this so called real world is a monumental difficulty, having to respond in certain ways to laws and regulations.

I am what they call a 'Medium', a 'Psychic', some might even say a witch. To me I am just me, complex, trying, honest and plain. When I link with beautiful Spirit, I come alive. They want nothing from me, only my time of which I have little, my truth and my god-given gift to help others.

Only problem is, not everyone wants to be helped! I try each day to give back but feel that my success rate on a scale of 0-10 is around 5.

Born to my poor unsuspecting parents, I was a tiny bundle of screams and strength. From birth I didn't sleep, keeping my parents on a constant vigil day and night, trying their hardest to figure out this child. Nothing would pacify me, only the hugs of my parents. I didn't take long to learn to walk, only to want to go in the opposite direction to everybody else. No-one understood me. I would talk to nothing and nobody, that nobody else could see anyway. I hated school and did not want to learn, knowing that all I needed was inside me. I rebelled against everything and everyone, wanting one thing in my life, love. Love for me, love for who I was. Very difficult when I pushed everyone away. I was always afraid of the dark, not wanting to be left to see and hear the voices.

I became a nuisance, defying all laws and authority. My poor Mum felt at times that she wanted to give up with me, but wouldn't, saying, 'Karen's just different.' Some places I refused point blank to enter, feeling the presence of negativity and anger. I revelled in enjoying the laughter and fun only I could see and hear.

All through my life I have had to fight against anything and everything that didn't sit right with me, which in turn lead me to a path of loneliness.

Over the years I have cried many tears of pain and frustration, only to feel no relief when they finally stopped running down my cheeks.

I adored my Grandpa, a man who could talk and link to all animals including birds. A big gentle man, who would talk and guide me through my younger years. His death when I was 26 destroyed me, my heart broke into tiny pieces and my anger at Spirit was immense. I decided to block everything and not listen to them. Soon they stopped communicating, but never stopped loving me. I carried on, married with two beautiful children to love.

But once again my torment got the better of me and I went on a wild destructive spree, destroying my marriage, leaving my beautiful children and trying to find a purpose to everything within myself. Eventually I became so ill, and nearly died.

From that moment on my life changed. I was brought back to this world to do a job. To help as many people as possible, to use and spread my gift.

In doing this I was warned some will never understand the work, others will love it. Never ever stray from who you are, Karen. Accept your gifts, give the love to others; never, ever expect anything back for yourself.

So my life started all over again, only this time I wanted to be happy within myself, not hiding from who I am and what I can do.

Although my actions leaving the marital home pained and hurt my adorable children so much, they never turned their backs on me. I often wonder how two such beautiful souls could suffer so much pain at their mother leaving yet still love me.

Our relationship now is amazing and I have four beautiful grandchildren. Three boys to my daughter Emma and her husband David, and a daughter to my son Adam and his wife Victoria.

Alfie, my Angel	8 years old.
Louie, my Star	6 years old.
Freddie, my Sunshine	18 months old.
Evelyn, my Rainbow	7 months old.

They are my chance all over again. I adore them all, and each and every one of them has a piece of my heart.

Chapter One

The Beginning

Born 14th July 1957 to Wendy and Charles.
Respectable couple making their way in life. My
Father was in the Royal Navy and my Mother had
been a telephonist. Childhood Sweethearts.

I came into the world five-and-a-half pounds of
screaming trouble. I didn't sleep for more that 20
minutes at a time, day or night, until the age of
two, and then I had a fit. Doctors were called and
Phenobarbital was given to slow me down. It
knocked me out, stopping the voices for a while.
Over the years of learning what I have from Spirit,
I realised I had no desire to be back on this earth
plane and its dense energy, but I had made a choice
to return to do the work.

My Mother nurtured and loved me while never
understanding my anger and frustration as a child.
My father despaired of me at times, but loved me
anyway. They wondered if placing me in a psychiatric
hospital for children might help, but my Mum was
certain I would change eventually.

When I was three years old, my Mum gave birth to my brother Ross. He was such a good boy, loved by everyone, he was more passive than me.

I felt I needed to protect him from the bad, but didn't know how to do it. He was very sensitive and needed lots of hugs, whereas I would mostly shun human contact, unless it was my Grandpa. I felt great peace, love and warmth with him. My Grandma was a strong woman with high standards, and when she got cross my Grandpa would smile at me, reassuring me all the time.

At the age of five, living in a beautiful village called Shaftesbury in Dorset, I would walk a mile to visit a Roman Burial Ground. The ladies on the desk in a little kiosk would let me in and I would sit in awe in these ruins, listening and talking to people I thought were alive, just like me. My Dad would be sent to find me, he knew where to come, but never understood my fascination with the place.

When I was on my own I felt safe. It was the living that un-nerved me. I felt threatened by them, seeing their faces change into other faces, ugly and distorted, showing their true nature. Of course, not all were like that, some shone with light and beauty.

Spirit visited me regularly and I would talk about

them, only to be smiled at. The common quote was, 'How strange Karen is. What is she talking about?'

At the age of 10 we as a family went on a hugely life-changing trip to Hong Kong for my father's job. Mum, Dad, me and Ross. My heart broke as I left my Grandpa behind to embark on this amazing new life.

The journey in 1967 was a long and arduous one, but adventure was on the horizon. The heat when we arrived hit us like a whirlwind, it was hard to breathe, and my mother was scared for our safety as bombing and unrest were everywhere. We settled in with an amazing flat, school and life that we had never known existed.

I loved school in Hong Kong, for it was short days and long hours spent near the sea during term time. The island fascinated me and I took to life there as if I belonged. Much to my parents' despair I would catch a bus into the forbidden zone and barter with the locals for shoes and clothing. The bustle of life amazed me and for the first time I felt at one with the energy.

My youngest brother Nigel was born in Hong Kong and I adored him. We all did, he was such a happy soul with strength that none could see apart from me. He reminded me of my Grandpa, gentle and strong, so life fell into a happy place for three years, and then we had to come back to the UK.

As we landed terror struck again. I remember getting off the plane, and feeling so unhappy, seeing people with their bad energy all around me. I could see the Angels telling me to rise above it. Angels are beautiful creatures who come to the aid of us all every day to help and guide us. Our thoughts can be their messages, if only we would let them in.

I was happy seeing my Grandpa and Grandma again, and Uncle Alan, their son. Grandpa's big strong arms wrapped around me and gave me the comfort I needed.

It is true that I seemed strange to many people, the girl that would sit on large grave stones and talk, seemingly to myself. They didn't know I could see who I was talking to. I was the girl who shied away from physical touch, preferring to talk to our pets. The girl who hated school and would go against the grain, but was terrified of upsetting certain people in authority.

My life was complex, and as I got older and started to develop into a teenager it became even more difficult. I was 13 years old when we came back to England, a girl whose body was developing at a rapid rate and I hated it. I had long dark curly hair, which really was my crowning glory and great for me to hide behind. My Mum always wanted me to look girly and clean. I never did, preferring to dress in oversized clothes and be as messy as possible.

My Dad's job was with the Government and we went to live in Bletchley, Buckinghamshire. I hated the place, it was dense and dirty and angry. I started high school dressed in a short skirt, jumper, new midi-coat and patent boots. I was immediately disliked by nearly everybody. I hated every minute of school and would cry myself to sleep at night, wanting someone to hear me.

Spirit would try to comfort me but my sorrow was too great. Two months into my new school year I was set on by six girls who beat me up badly, ripping my new coat and pulling my hair out. They were about to bring a house brick down on my head when a lady's voice said, 'What are you doing? Leave her alone.' (An Earth Angel.) These girls ran so fast in fear. The woman smiled at me and picked me up.

I realised then that Spirit had saved me for the fourth time in my 13 years. First time was when I was five years old. I stepped out in front of a lorry and ended up underneath it, unmarked and unscathed, much to my parents' relief.

Second time was being pulled into a lake by a boy aged seven, and nearly drowning, only to be brought to the surface by my Dad, not breathing. I suddenly took a breath and sat up crying because my Daddy couldn't heave himself up out of the water.

The third time was in Hong Kong, where we weren't supposed to venture into the Chinese quarter because it was dangerous. I did, and was lead by an Angel to safer ground when a fight broke out and I was in the centre of it.

The fourth time, walking home from my new school to my parents' house beaten, scared and my new coat ripped to pieces, I felt so alone, even Spirit's kind words couldn't help. Why was I so different? Why did people want to hurt me? Why did I have to live in Bletchley, or even England, come to that?

I started to hate myself. Stupid, stupid me, I struggled with school work, hating all of it apart from English and R.E., where I could express myself and excel because of my love for Jesus, God and Mother Mary.

My Dad was a very proud, hard-working man, and when he saw me walk into the house black and blue, coat torn, his anger at who had hurt me was immense. After all, no matter how different I was,

I was his daughter and he loved me. He wanted to go up to the school to complain, but I was terrified of being weak and hurt again. So he showed me how to retaliate, first picking on the leader of the group by confronting her with words and a twist of the wrist. It worked, no more fear for me.

My life started to change. I became the leader of the group, defiant, causing mayhem in class, always in detention. My motto, to be one step ahead always. For several years I carried on living the school girl life, with a boyfriend in tow, being a nightmare, and always in trouble.

I was thrown out of school at 15 and became a trainee telephonist, something I mastered within weeks, but once again my defiant nature took over and I stopped going to work, intent on finding a quiet place to just be alone and talk to my Angels and Spirit, longing for some peace within and to not always be battling with who I was.

Spirit would talk to me continually, warning me of trouble ahead. I was always one step ahead of the law and my Dad, who continually tried to understand this wild daughter of his, said I was a black widow spider, drawing people in and then devouring them, spitting them out when I no longer needed them.

This of course was not true. People were drawn

to me, good and bad. I tried to help, but was very naive about the true power of my gifts. I went along with the bad as well as the good and would always land myself in trouble to protect others.

Chapter Two

The Teenage Years

I badly wanted to be good, to be right in my actions, but try as I might, I never managed to be the calm, quiet person my parents wanted so much. My Mum and Dad kept trying with me, but they had difficulties with money in the early 1970s and my Mum eventually went into a state of depression.

My parents tried to hide this from us three children, but I knew what was happening. I so wanted to hold my Mum in my arms and take away her darkness. Every night I asked the Angels to help her. I wanted to talk to her, but how could they know that a 13 year old girl had enough knowledge inside her to help at that time.

Eventually my Mum's happiness started to return and we carried on with family life, with me becoming more and more interested in boys. But once again, never the good boys, only the strange troubled ones. My first boyfriend had long blonde hair down his back, the fashion at the time. He was gentle and kind, coming from a hard background with a father who lashed him with a belt and a mother who just didn't care. I loved his gentleness, but fought against his love, not letting him close.

I was fiercely independent and determined to go my own way, wild and totally crazy. With long dark curly hair and deep brown eyes, I cared for no-one. The living always wanted to change me, whereas Spirit accepted me and tried to guide me.

It was around this time that I started to see darker energy, Spirit that appeared friendly, but with false smiles. This is when the nightmares began. Spirit came to me day and night, something I was used to, but the darker energies would leave shadows behind on ceilings and walls, leaving me too terrified to sleep without the light on.

My Mum and Dad always kept a constant vigil over me, Mum always trying to find my happiness, Dad with his reasonable and competent way of dealing with me.

One night I decided to stay out all night, not telling my parents. My father's job was quite an important one, and there was always a fear at the back of his mind that one of us could be kidnapped or harmed in some way. That night – at the age of 14 – when I didn't come home, was a night of sheer terror for them. Believing I had been kidnapped, the police kept a constant watch at our home.

At around 9 o'clock the next morning, I walked in all unsuspecting, to be met by the police and questioned for over an hour as to my whereabouts.

My parents' faces said it all, and I felt their pain hit me in the heart full force. What had I done? My Mum's tears flowed and she didn't know whether to hug me or tell me off. I felt so, so sad and ashamed at my thoughtlessness.

I heard the Angels asking me to look at my Mum and see her pain. I ran to my bedroom, hating myself more than ever. Why did I have to challenge everything? Why did I hear all these voices? Why could I not live like other children did? I was angry at Spirit, the good loving Spirit, and the blameless Angels for not guiding me. Not realising these were my lessons to learn, I let in the dark and began to lead a life of danger and destruction in every way for the next four years. (I realise now that I had to see this side, to be able to do the work I do today.)

I went to work when I felt like it, learning fast and then not turning up, running around with lost souls, people with no desire to live a good life. I became a hippy, my light side still fighting to regain control of the darker side. I didn't participate in any form of drug taking, as others did. I really could not understand why anybody would want to let a substance control them. Once again the Angels guided me through the most dangerous of situations, keeping me safe. So many times I put myself in danger, but was always protected.

I started to cover my body in loose clothing, dark colours, looking menacing in every way, but my heart always remained pure and true.

At fifteen I met a boy called Graham and fell totally in love, an all encompassing love. I knew him inside out and would do anything to keep him happy. He was three years older than me and our parents met each other.

I started working for his father's company in the office. I held the records of every member of staff and felt so important. I could look at those records and know who was lying and who wasn't, just by touching the words. I dressed smartly and for the first time felt I was normal, but I wasn't.

All the time, I was being talked to by these people's deceased relatives, and I didn't know what to do with the messages I was getting. So I would smile at the people who needed help, make them tea or coffee and touch their hand as I felt it was the right thing to do. For a few months I was happy and then things started to go wrong.

One of my main problems has been that I trust everybody, always trying to find the good in people. I never recognized my own beauty, my seductiveness or the fact that I fascinated people, always hiding behind my hair.

About this time I started to go and watch live bands. Genesis, David Bowie, Black Sabbath, the list goes on. My Dad would drop me off at these gigs, and I would meet up with Graham and others, then went inside, ear drums bombarded with loud music, loving the energy and people enjoying themselves.

I would come out deafened, and Dad would be there to pick me up. He never wanted me to travel with anybody else, just wanting to keep me safe. On one of those nights I begged him to let me come home with friends. He reluctantly agreed, after much pleading from me.

Two lads that worked in Graham's father's business offered to take me home. I knew them and trusted them. Luton to Bletchley is not far. So I got in their van. As we set off, five minutes into the journey, I felt this terrible fear envelop me.

'Oh God please help me,' I thought. 'Stop the van please, I need to get out.' The two lads stopped on a grass verge, and fear took over. I was attacked by both. I remember stepping out of my body and watching the whole event. One had a knife.

'Am I going to die?' I asked Spirit.

'No,' was the reply, 'but look at your eyes, little one, you are an empty body. You must learn not to trust all, you must learn that there is bad out there, not all people can be helped.'

With that I entered my body and was getting up. They had finished with me. I got back in the van and was dropped off at home, told to keep my mouth shut. Nobody would believe me anyway. I walked into my home smiling at my Mum and Dad. Then I ran upstairs and the pain hit me full force.

I went into the bathroom, washed myself, and cried and cried. The Angels tried to console me, but I wouldn't let them near. I felt nothing, I felt everything. God, why have you done this, please somebody tell me. Nothing came back and I felt so betrayed.

I went in to work the next day and came face to face with my abusers. This went on for three weeks. I told nobody but eventually plucked up courage to tell Graham's father. I begged him not to tell my Dad or Mum. I could not deal with their pain, only my own.

Graham's father confronted these lads and fired them. They had no work thereafter, finding life very difficult. Spirit told me how brave I was. This was one of many things I would experience in my younger years. I can speak of these events now, realizing that to do my job properly, to be able to connect with people from the heart, not only would I need to access my Spiritual gift properly, I would also need to work from life experiences.

I felt very vulnerable after my experience, and could not get close to anybody after being attacked. I loved being around my brothers and wanted to spend time safe in my own home. Graham soon started to cheat on me, and one of our friends died in a terrible accident. Another friend told me Graham was cheating on me with his partner. I was heartbroken, confronted them and ended the relationship.

During this time my parents moved to Cheltenham. Once again I felt alone in a new town. I started working and loved my job in a sports shop. Graham wanted me back. I left home for a while before working in the sports shop, living rough, experiencing so many of life's lessons, only to come back home to Cheltenham at 18, wiser, older and wanting to get on with a normal life. But Spirit would not let me stop. At night they would arrive by my bed talking, and as my nights merged into days, I found Spirit to be a valuable part of my every day existence, warning me when danger lurked and helping me to smile, even when I felt down.

Mum and Dad on honeymoon.

Mum and Dad in Hong Kong.

My Granddad,
with whom I felt
so safe.

Me at 6 years old.
Butter wouldn't melt!

Grandma and Grandpa with my brother at 10 months, and me at the age of three.

Mum with my brother and me.

Mum with my younger brother in Hong Kong.

Chapter Three

Normal!!

My Mum and Dad welcomed me back with open arms, Dad comforting me late into the night when my tears would fall, not really knowing why I was crying, he helped me to feel strong again. I soon settled into my new job, loving the feel of being important, printing T-shirts for the college, meeting new people.

It was here that I met my husband to be. Eleven years older than me, he struck me as so sure of himself, good job, kind, caring and honest. We started dating. I think I was in awe of him at the beginning. He wanted to be with me, he liked my different ways and my vulnerability. I was such a free Spirit, loving the sun, cheese cloth clothing and freedom, leaving my hair long and wild, my eyes brown and soulful, and I loved to smile and laugh.

Richard cared for me and my parents were delighted that at last I was with a caring, present-able man. We got engaged and planned our wedding.

Not once did I tell him that I talked to Spirit every day and night. It was at this time that the voices started to stop. I felt normal. We got married on 1st October 1977.

Everything had gone wrong leading up to the wedding. My Mum was taken in to hospital very poorly, and was only allowed out for my special day. High on valium, she didn't really know what was going on. My Dad sold his car to help pay for the wedding. I was really ready for the day, feeling beautiful and special, but wondered was this right, am I worthy enough?

We settled down to family life and our first baby was born on 29th March 1979. After a long hard labour, Emma came into the world, so beautiful and perfect, and screaming her head off. I was 21 years old and scared stiff but loved my baby so much. Four years later our son was born. Weighing 10 lbs 2 ozs, he shot into the world, strong and silent. He was my beautiful frog, changing into a handsome prince as he grew. I loved my children with all my heart and soul, and I put everything into being the perfect wife and mother.

But I always felt Spirit calling me, I tried not to listen but knew when danger was around. People were amazed when I stopped them from going to certain places, only to discover that where they were intending to be, there had been a terrible accident. I tried so hard to be conventional, but just couldn't. I loved to dance and sing with my children, and collected stray dogs and cats, re-homing them for their own safety in our home, much to my husband's despair.

I spent the next eight years living the best I could between two worlds, being at home with my family, playing at being the perfect housewife. My husband was a good man; he provided for us and loved us with all his heart. I knew Spirit was leaving me alone to do what was important in my heart, to live the life I so wanted as a Mum, wife and daughter that I tried so hard to be. I always felt love, that didn't ever leave me, and I tried to live my life with love every day.

My parents moved to Cyprus in 1985 and as a family we decided to go there on holiday for a month. I was so excited. A week before we were due to leave, I came out in red weals all over my body, they looked like whip marks, so I made a trip to the doctor. He had no idea what they were, but said I should take anti-histamines, which I did.

We landed in Cyprus, met by my Dad, my husband Richard, our children Emma and Adam aged 6 and 2, and me. The heat hit us and I felt very strange, like I was coming home. We went to my parents' house and I loved being there, but felt ill immediately with sickness, a high temperature and the red marks getting worse. I had to stay in the house for a week and a half, eventually feeling well enough to venture out.

I knew Cyprus immediately. I knew where I was, and had flash backs of being whipped and beaten. The people of Cyprus told me I was one of them, even changing my name to Katarina instead of Karen. Everywhere I went they spoke to me in Greek. I loved my time there, it felt like home.

The family had an amazing month, and when we came back to England, I felt the oppression once again. Tears rolled down my face. I was so unhappy and cold, even though it was summer.

Not long afterwards, I received a terrible phone call from my Mother that my Grandpa had died. When told of his death I collapsed into a heap on the floor, and my husband tried in vain to comfort me. I felt as though my heart had been ripped out. My Mum came home and we went to see him laid to rest. He looked so, so beautiful, I kissed his cheek and heard his voice behind me saying, 'I am still here, Karen.'

I was so angry at his death, and refused to listen to Spirit, selfishly asking, 'How could you take away this beautiful light, the only person who had ever seen the real me?'

I started to dislike Winchcombe, the place we lived as a family and, for no real reason, set about finding another place for us to live. We moved to Evesham, back to my husband's home town, and I loved our house. But where ever I went, I always felt animosity towards me. I just didn't fit in, but once again set about being as normal as I could. My feelings when danger arrived didn't stop and I was able to protect my family.

My children have always been my life, even when my marriage started to go wrong. I felt driven to do things that weren't right. I started up a business with a good friend, a fast food van that was fun and hard work, but it put a wedge between my husband and me.

I felt compelled to go against everyone and everything. I had to keep moving forward, as if I was being drawn by something or someone to be a success, but nothing I did gave me pleasure or satisfaction. My marriage started to fall apart and I wouldn't listen to anybody, I had to keep going.

It was at this time I met a man called Steve.

He seemed to offer something more in my life. I started an affair, something I am not proud of, but I felt nothing at all inside for him. I just kept going. He was eventually killed in a terrible car crash. I woke up at around 3 o'clock in the morning and knew he was dead. I heard his footsteps outside and looked out but saw no-one. I felt him near me, and I was told at 9 a.m. next day that he was dead.

Then started a string of events. I felt nothing, only emptiness. It turned out he had been seeing several other women. We all bought the same flowers for his funeral, which was strange as none of us new about the others. I just carried on trying to re-build my marriage, but it was too late, I had done too much damage.

After another two years I left our marital home and moved in with a new man I'd met called Kevin. At this time I was causing so much pain to others and I started to feel very alone. My children stayed with their father and my heart broke every day with pain. I loved them so much, but knew I couldn't take them from their Daddy. He was and still is a good man and father, and I was a total mess, mixed up and driven. I stopped eating, driving myself to the verge of anorexia, and my body started to close down.

I experienced so much hurt, pain and destruction, never finding happiness, yet all these experiences have since helped me to help others. So my life took a new course of events. One relationship led to another, one disappointment to another. I worked so hard with so little reward, and I cried tears of regret and sadness. Eventually, after a prolapse of the bowel, I started to eat properly again. Another punishment brought on myself.

At the age of 40, on January 4th 1998, a Sunday, I was working, managing a sports bar in the Cheltenham area, my son Adam was with me, and I started to feel ill and so cold. The bar was very quiet and after doing my usual jobs in the morning, I went and sat with my back to the radiator, thinking I must have been hit by a nasty bout of flu. By 1 p.m. I felt very poorly and by 3 p.m. I asked my son to ring my partner at that time, to come and fetch us.

I managed to close the sports club bar with help from my son who was 14 years old at the time. By 4 p.m. my temperature was through the roof and I was delirious. I had been suffering with a lung infection previous to this, and thought perhaps it hadn't cleared properly. I remember feeling so ill,

I lay down on my sofa and drifted in and out of sleep. By 10 p.m. I started to hurt, all my joints were in so much pain and my head felt like it was going to explode. By 1 a.m. I was being violently sick, crawling to the bathroom because I couldn't walk.

At 5 a.m. I was shaking so much, my son came out of his bedroom, looked at me and the blotches on my arms and legs, and said, 'You have meningitis, Mum, please phone the hospital.'

His words hit me hard. By now I was in the worst pain and couldn't focus properly. Toxic septicaemia had started to race through my body. After first making sure my son was okay for school, I managed to struggle downstairs and was driven to the local hospital in Evesham.

Very soon a doctor arrived, tried to lift my arm and I screamed in agony. I had never felt pain like it. My head was in agony, as was the rest of my body. I was rushed to Worcester Hospital by ambulance and a specialist was brought in to assess me. After a lumbar puncture I was diagnosed with Meningococcal C and Toxic Septicaemia, isolated and placed in intensive care. My family were called. They were told on a scale of 1-10, 10 being death, I was a 9. They were told I was dying. I had five lines going into a main artery, blood being taken from everywhere and anywhere as my veins had collapsed. My organs were ready to shut down and my head had swollen. At this time I didn't know who was alive and who was dead around me. I kept drifting in and out of consciousness. Nobody could come near me without a mask on.

Mum and Dad collected my daughter Emma to visit me. She was 18 years old at the time. They wouldn't let Adam in to see me, it was felt it would be too distressing for him. Emma has since told me that when she sat with me, I said I wanted my Mummy, as if I was a little girl again. My Mother refused to accept I had meningitis and told doctors and nurses I was not dying.

I remember the vicar standing at the end of my bed as I drifted again. All of a sudden, I was floating down a blue tunnel feeling very happy. Then I was thrown into white light, and in front of me I saw my Grandpa standing beside a tree. He looked about 30 years old. I ran towards him and his arms opened wide.

To this day I have never felt love like I did then, or so much peace. He talked to me so gently about the family and I asked him, 'Where are we going?' He replied, 'You have to go back, Karen.'

I begged him, 'Please no, let me stay with you.'

He smiled and said, 'No, you have work to do. You will be shown, Karen, you must go now. I will see you again.'

My heart started to break and all of a sudden I felt a rush around me and I opened my eyes with a gasp, trying desperately to remove the oxygen mask from my face. Doctors and nurses were everywhere around me. An Angel (nurse) helped me remove the mask. I looked at her and said, 'I don't need it any more.' She smiled at me and said, 'Just a bit longer,' and I fell asleep.

When I awoke the time on the clock was 10.30 a.m., the same time as when I had entered intensive care, only now it was two days later. My recovery was about to begin. I don't think I have ever felt such overall pain in my body as I did then. I tried to move but just felt pain, and the buzzing in my head would not stop. After five days I was in an isolation room on a ward.

Every time I woke from sleep, my Dad was sitting next to me, willing me to live. I could feel his strength and love every minute of every day. My Mum still would not accept my meningitis, saying that I was very very ill, but I would survive.

Soon they allowed people in to see me, watching people's faces turn to horror as they looked at me.

Thin, with open sores on my legs from the septicaemia and my head looked out of proportion to the rest of me. I was not allowed to look in the mirror, and did not want to. I did not want any help to sit on a commode, but didn't have much choice to start with.

Days went by, and at night I would see endless dark shadows coming towards me and then drift away with a screeching in my head. Sometimes I would see light shining brightly at the door and a feeling of peace would come over me. At first I could only crawl to the toilet, but I was determined and would not let my Mum help me in the hospital. I started to bed bath myself, each day getting stronger. The first time I was allowed to have a shower I was delighted, but had to be helped as I had no strength.

Then came the tests done by various doctors in their chosen field. They could not believe how quickly I was starting to recover, and when they checked the flow of blood around my body they were totally shocked, as I apparently had the blood flow of an athlete, not somebody who had toxic septicaemia. I so wanted to go home, and six weeks after I was taken into hospital I was released into the care of my parents.

Slowly I started to get stronger, but my head never stopped ringing, and I kept going over and over my teeming thoughts.

Night after night my Mum would sit with me as I held my head and cried. All of a sudden it stopped and I started to feel whole again. So scared of living again, frightened to touch anything that belonged to someone else, frightened of the outside world and its dangers.

I had changed. I was different. I became even crazier than I was before. Testing everything and realizing that I had a purpose, a meaning. But what? What was I going to do?

I went back to work part-time and met a girl called Dawn at an interview. I knew straight away she was to be a part of my life from that point, a beautiful person who became such a close friend.

She introduced me to a Healer and Medium to help me after the doctor had signed me off, and said I should get some alternative medicine to help with the rest of my healing. And so the next part of my spiritual and earthly journey began.

Chapter Four

My Spiritual Work Begins

Meeting Dawn's Healer and Medium started me on the path to believing in myself, who I am and what I was meant to be doing with my life. The moment I walked into her home she asked me if I knew how spiritual I was.

'Yes,' I said, 'but I am not interested in knowing more. I have come here for help with healing.' She said okay, but if I wanted to think about developing my spirituality in the future, to let her know.

Spirit would not stop telling me to join her development group, so I did. I was amazed to discover I could give others in the group messages from Spirit. Members of their families who had died, wanted to let their loved ones know they were still around and okay. They told me things that nobody could know apart from them and their family. I started passing on these messages and loved how I was working and listening to Spirit. Learning how to open and close my chakra points, how to meditate in order to connect and visualise, to sit and be at peace with Spirit.

I must say though, I found it hard to quieten my mind, to hear Spirit clearly after years of hearing them all talking at once.

A few months after joining the group, I felt this strong presence beside me. The energy of this Spirit was pressing down on my head and chest and I felt compelled to have him near. He kept coming in and working with me. One evening I asked his name. 'Rising Sun, Child,' came the reply.

A Sioux Indian! Old and proud with a large hook nose and rugged, weathered skin, with gentleness and love for me. 'I am your guide and I am honoured to be here,' he said. 'I will work with you. I have always worked with you and I will always do so in the future. Now is your time, Child. Now to do the work.'

I soon realised that it was Rising Sun who delivered all Spirit messages to me. He is my Guide, my Spiritual protector and I love and trust him unconditionally. With his help, I learnt how to control my gift in the right way, to be precise and professional with the work and readings I was giving. I learnt so much from the lady who lead the Group, I sat in with them and was soon working for her in her business.

At last I began to see myself as a Medium, and to refer to myself as a Medium. Soon people were booking with me to have readings. I work from my heart, and was told by my mentor that she could see all the energy floating from my heart, pink energy, surrounding and helping people. I loved what I was doing and realised that here was my niche, this was what I was meant to do. There was no fear involved, just pleasure from giving so much, until one day a man came to see me. I picked up danger around him in his long black coat and he looked unusual.

Rising Sun told me to be careful with the reading and to be gentle. Don't linger too long on any one thing. I took his advice and discovered from this client's Grandfather who had passed over, that he liked knives a little bit too much. Although I was un-nerved I remained calm and gave a reading, even talking about knives. He left happy.

It was the start of my learning many lessons, that I cannot trust everyone, and to remember to always listen and trust my gut instinct. I started to become stronger with myself, energy building, and feeling so alive and well.

I lived in a flat at this time and loved going home to meditate and to talk to Spirit. My children accepted what I was doing, and I believe they were glad that I had at last discovered a direction. As for the rest of my family, I am sure they thought I had gone more mad than ever, but they went along with what was happening. I learnt how to channel energy through my body, to heal with my voice and hands. I was at last using the gift I had been given, I was no longer useless and strange, I had a gift, a real gift and I was able to use it.

At last all the things I had been through, all my anger, pain and solitude, began to make sense. I felt every day that I was on the path to something good, and I learnt so much. I started to learn how to release trapped spirits to the other side. Ones that won't budge, or feel safer in the house they have always known. Encouraging them to see the light and to know that it's okay to leave. And I learnt how to protect myself from Spiritual attack.

It is very true that many people do not want to believe or have anything to do with Spiritual experiences and I respect that. Everything is free choice and I would never want to try and push this work on anybody, believer or not, but it does sadden me that some people are so nasty and verbally cruel towards Mediums. As Rising Sun says, 'They can see only what is in front of them, Child. Do not be saddened by this, it is just how it is.'

I knew that if only people would give up on greed and power, they would be able to see beauty in the smallest of things, in a smile, a tear, strength and honesty, but most of all love.

Rising Sun was and still is so patient with me, teaching me to listen, feel and see a person's inner self, what lies beneath the surface, and to be patient (the hardest thing to learn) as the human body and mind wants everything given to us **now,** often forgetting that if you keep trying, in the end your patience will pay off and you will receive. Maybe not in the way you thought you wanted, but it is there for you.

More and more people were coming to me to hear messages from their loved ones who had passed over, and these beautiful Spirits would give me details and messages that could only be known to their loved ones still living. To me, every person that comes to see me is special, alive or dead.

I started to realise that there was so much more to this work than just listening to messages, putting them together piece by piece, and delivering them in a compassionate and loving way. It is also about guiding the person to happiness in their own life, to help them to fulfil their own potential in whatever way they want to.

Every day I was learning, and I still am. I realised one day that I had to be professional about this work, after I gave a message to a young man as he was working in a pub. It was a message from his Grandmother that he hadn't even asked for. She was asking me to tell him that she loved those large yellow daisies with the black centre, and that he didn't need to worry, she knew he loved her even though he had told his Dad he didn't want to go to her funeral because she had not given him the same amount of pocket money as she had given his sister. The poor lad dropped the glass he was holding, tears in his eyes and fled.

I felt so awful, and I couldn't find him to explain. Rising Sun said, 'Another lesson, Child. Be careful with your gift. You have to be professional about this and in control of when and how you use it.' Lesson learnt.

Also, in my experience, Spirit and drinking spirits do not mix. When I have a drink, I no longer have control over the link between Spirit and myself. I now know to explain this first, that I won't be giving or receiving any messages while I am enjoying myself having a drink.

I loved being able to help the living to realise that although their family, lover, child or friend had passed over, they were still around to help, love and guide them.

All of my experiences in life so far had been preparing me for this work. All the happiness, the many jobs, hurt, anger, and plain stupidity had brought me to this and I no longer felt alone.

People from all walks of life were coming to see me and I gave all I could in the messages. Things were getting better. I learnt about signs from Spirit such as white feathers falling in front of you, or finding them in your car or home. They are messages of love from the Angels or a Spirit being.

I started to feel touch over my hands from Spirit, but now I wasn't afraid. My trust in Rising Sun grew and grew, he would talk to me day and night whenever I needed questions answered. Often I would have to work at getting the full message by asking more questions.

I still have to go through life with all its ups and downs, but I started to realise that most of the downs were of my choosing, and that if I wanted the good and happiness in my life, then I had to make it happen. Us humans have one big fault, we expect the best just because as far as we are concerned we should have it. Yet every time we put a negative out there with our minds, for example,

'Nothing is going right, I hate my life, I can't be bothered, it's his/her fault this happened, I never have any money', that is what we keep attracting to ourselves. Unfortunately this is what society has been thinking and doing for eons and it is difficult to change. But in my experience, by putting a positive mindset out into the universe, that is what you get back, positivity and progress.

After I had sold my flat and paid off my debts, I moved into a small home with a partner (another learning curve). The place we moved to was rented, a lovely little building on a farm. I really did like this place, set in the countryside. Spirit was visiting me regularly and I loved talking to them day in day out, and working with them. Life seemed to fall into place but I still had a niggling feeling within my soul that this relationship was wrong. He was cheating on me regularly and I tried to stop the messages coming to me in feelings and words about his infidelity. Maybe this was Karma for all the pain I had caused my ex-husband? All I knew was that I had to keep going and that it would come to a head. I just didn't realise how my life would be affected while all this was going on.

Emma and Adam enjoyed coming to our little house and spending evenings there with us and friends. One night we had been out to the local pub, came home and were sitting chatting, when I glanced in the mirror and saw a Spirit coming down the stairs. Nothing unusual for me, but he was dressed in white robes and had a beard. He looked like one of the disciples.

What I didn't realise was that my daughter had seen him too. Suddenly her voice broke. 'Oh my god, look, look!' and she started to cry. So did the others. Then my son saw it too, and his friends, and panic started to grow. 'It's okay,' I said, 'it's okay, he's not here to hurt you.' In fact he was beautiful. He didn't speak, he just stood on the stairs.

My daughter did see Spirits from time to time, and didn't really like it, they un-nerved her. The Spirit then disappeared and I hadn't asked why he was there, and we carried on. If only I had asked, maybe I could have done something there and then for someone I loved, but I know now that he was there to show his love and support for the coming year.

Around this time we had a Medium come to my place of work to do readings all day. She was well known and very good in her profession. She had no idea that I was a Medium too, and I went in to see her first. She looked at my palms and said, 'You are a Medium and your life is going to be amazing. Through your work you will travel far and are blessed, people will want to see you and will need your guidance and love.'

She also told me things about my life and family that were spot on. Then she said, 'I have to give this message, one of your parents is going to die within the next year.' I looked at her stunned and started to say no no, thinking of my father. 'Listen,' she said, 'you will have to help your family, you have to be told and this is not something that I am normally given.'

I heard myself saying, 'My Father?' but she said, 'No, your Mother. Your father's heart will break.'

I looked at her. 'No,' I said, 'you must be wrong. My Mum is so full of life and a very busy lady.'

Her face suddenly came into my mind. My Mum? No, that won't happen.

I left with my tape, not wanting to talk to anyone. I went outside into the garden of the place where I worked and lit a cigarette. I was shaking, while my head was screaming, 'No! Not my beautiful Mum.'

The Medium had gone on to tell me that Mum would develop cancer, be diagnosed and die within three months. I was told this early in 2002. I could not tell anyone, I was in a state of shock and would not believe it. I asked Rising Sun but had no answer back, so as the days went by I put it to the back of my mind, but always looked at my Mum deeply to see if I could see any signs in her aura (energy field). I couldn't, so life carried on.

Over Christmas of that year Mum had very bad pains in her upper stomach and chest. She went to the doctor, had various tests and was told she had gall stones. January, February, March, April, more tests, admitted to hospital, out of hospital. At the end of April or early May 2003, I took Mum to the doctor where a locum doctor examined her tummy. She found a lump the size of an orange.

Mum sat with me in the car. 'I have cancer, don't I, Karen?' I just nodded my head and cried with her. 'I want to go home and see your Dad,' she said. I dropped her off and then broke my heart, screaming at Spirit NO NO NO.

More tests for my Mum brought a diagnosis of advanced pancreatic cancer. This was May, giving her three months to live. She told us all together, we told our children, who all loved her so much. I will never forget seeing the pain in my brothers and my Dad, not accepting this at all. I didn't know what to say or do. No tears would come, I felt empty. Please help me, Spirit, please help her.

What happened then was amazing. My Mum had so much dignity, she arranged her own funeral, sorted everything, even her jewellery, and tried her hardest through her pain to be strong for all of us. We all tried to carry on as normal.

Mum loved the sun and it shone day after day, meaning she could sit outside every day. Near my birthday in July I took her out to my place and on the way we saw a field of poppies. We stopped and just stood by the field taking in the colour and the energy. 'How beautiful,' she said, 'and so perfect. The colour, Karen, the colour.' On my birthday she gave me a card with poppies on. 'Our special thing,' she said, and it always has been since then.

She talked to all the grandchildren, gently confirming that she was not afraid and neither should they be. Not once did she complain about her illness or how she felt. On September 5th she passed away after a time in the Sue Ryder Hospice. We were with her and as she started to go I could see lights around her bed, energy was forming to take her, her Spirit family. I laid my head against her back feeling her physical body slipping away.

I couldn't cry, I had to keep strong for everyone, her especially. She was such an amazing person and as she was slipping away, I told her I could see her walking in between yellow roses. When she was cremated there were cushions of yellow roses behind her resting place. My pain was immense, I just wanted to run and run calling her name. 'I need you, please come back, please.' Nothing happened. I drove to an open place near where I lived, got out of the car and screamed, and my heart broke. It was at this point that I felt a presence behind me. I was in the middle of nowhere.

Rising Sun, my Guide, was standing next to me and I felt the arms of the being behind me gently come around me and hold me. I could hear the words, 'Hush, Child.' I realised I was making such a strange noise and I felt myself being held. It was the Spirit in robes that we had seen in the house, comforting me and gently talking to me.

Rising Sun told me Mum was resting and I saw a large room with no windows, but beautiful green grass and flowers outside, red and yellow, pink and blue. There were beds lined up with white sheets, and white linen curtains blowing in the breeze. Angels were everywhere, touching and healing the Spirits, the souls of people who had died. Family and friends of newly passed people, those who had passed over before them, were beside them, gently holding their hands. I felt so privileged to see this, and my tears stopped flowing.

About a week after Mum had passed, Emma and I went into the pub where my then partner worked as a chef, to have a drink. As we sat down, a young girl stood up and started to sing in the most beautiful voice, 'Fields of Gold', the song my Mum had chosen for her cremation. Emma and I looked at each other and the tears flowed. Mum was certainly letting us know she was still around, in whatever way she could.

I have seen Mum several times since her death, even showing me my own funeral. I was standing next to her, watching a very handsome young man in a suit who was upset in a church. I looked at my clothes and said to Mum, 'I don't like what I am wearing, and who is that handsome man?'

'It is Louie, your grandson. My great grandson, and you are wearing what they have chosen for you.'

'Why?' I asked.

'Because this is your funeral you are seeing.'

I then realised the rest of my deceased family were standing in the line with me. 'Thanks a lot, Mum,' I said. 'Not something I wish to see.' She just smiled at me.

As a family we all kept close after Mum's

passing, going out for walks and lunch on a Sunday with Dad, keeping a close eye on him, as his world had totally collapsed. My Mum and Dad first went out together when they were 15 years old, and had immense love for each other. His pain ran so deep. Spirit would talk to me day and night, helping me to help my family.

The work kept coming and I kept learning. I had experience after experience. My partner and I moved to Winchcombe but slowly our relationship dwindled because he was working away from home. Before we split up we went on holiday to Spain. I don't like flying, my balance goes and I feel very strange not being earthed. On the day we were due to fly I asked Rising Sun to help me with my fear. He looked so funny in full Indian headdress getting on the plane. When we took off he sat in the aisle saying, 'It is just a metal bird, Child,' and put his head through the window. With all of his playing around and making me laugh inside, we were soon landing, my fear had subsided.

I decided this holiday would be a healing process. The sun, sea and freedom were lovely, but I wanted my Mum and my family.

I felt lonely inside and terribly confused at this point, even with all I knew from Spirit, all the teachings I had been given, I still couldn't make sense of such a beautiful soul as my Mum being taken from us.

You see, Spirit had explained to me that as a Spirit, your soul chooses who you will be born to. You also know how you will die, and you accept that. Some people are very old souls who have been here time and time again, returning to learn the lessons we needed to learn from our past lives. But once back on an earthly level, we may have decided not to learn, and so we come back again and again to make our lives right and complete.

We may come back as a different sex – male or female – but we are drawn to the people whose souls we have met many times before. Some people are new souls starting their journey on this earth plane.

In the next chapter I will try to make this more understandable for people, to help them with their journey. I have been here many times and am still learning. Also, I do believe, and have been told by Rising Sun, that we do have a choice not to return. I just keep coming back, not content that I have done all I can to receive peace within my own soul.

Me aged three.

Me aged 15 with my brothers aged 12 and 4 years.

With my Mum in my early 20s.

My wedding day – 1st October, 1977.

My daughter in my arms at her Christening.

My son and daughter making a splash.

Great Grandpa and Grandma with my children, Adam and Emma.

Chapter Five

Life, and Returning
Time and Again

When a couple, male and female, decide to have a physical relationship, souls are deciding who their offspring should be born to. The soul enters the baby. I cannot explain how this happens, but as the embryo forms, the soul flourishes. The soul has chosen this journey. I have asked how this can be right when so many children and adults live awful lives or die terrible deaths. The reply from Spirit was, 'This is such a small part of the soul's existence. The human body is just an overcoat for this lifetime. The soul is the truth of a person, the thing that is trying so hard to give the body an insight into a beautiful life.' A very difficult thing to do, considering that earthly existence is so regimented and dense in energy.

'Look at babies, Child,' said Rising Sun. 'They come into this world pure, and so ready to feel love. It is love that warms them, causes them to smile and to feel safe. But see a child who has anger and pain in its life, and they look away in fear and silence.

As a soul, how can they believe in better or understand love? Yet they keep trying, because as a soul they do know what unconditional love is. That is why they continue to feel love for their abuser.

'The purest of beings, babies feel only love and hunger from within. Feeling pain and anger are learned on the physical plane.'

I have tried to make sense of this many times, when I have watched so much pain coursing through people's bodies due to the loss of a loved one. But I know that offering words of explanation and comfort can help so many people to rid themselves of guilt and pain over the death of someone they loved so much.

I realise that not everyone can accept this explanation, but it seems that the saying 'Only the good die young' does make some sense of the explanation that living your life with unconditional love, and caring for others, enables you to feel more at peace just before your death. Your soul is the part of you that knows no boundaries where unconditional love is concerned. The more you allow yourself to just be in the moment, the more you can feel the presence of your soul.

It has taken me many years of searching to realise that I am who I have made myself to be. To accept yourself for who you are, to delve deep into your inner self to question the things your earthly self does that you do not really like; and the things you see in others, such as deceit, anger, jealousy, greed, suffering, victimization, these are things to let go of and to change. No-one decides your happiness for you. Only you can do that.

Look at all your positive attributes and feelings – love, warmth, generosity, caring, laughter and understanding. These qualities are your soul talking to you, a feeling from within you. Let them flourish within to guide you and help you feel more at peace, at one with yourself.

Loving yourself for all your goodness and being is not a selfish act, it is necessary for a less troubled existence. Being who you truly want to be will live through your soul's purpose. Smile at people even when you feel unable to. This not only warms their heart and soul, but yours too.

It is our choice to make this a good life for ourselves with all its twists and turns. Allow your soul to be in harmony with your earthly self to receive the many things this earth has to offer with LOVE.

Chapter Six

Patience

I kept looking for my Mum, calling to her night after night, but she seemed to have gone. I was told by Rising Sun to let her rest. 'She will speak soon enough, Child.'

I realised then that I was being selfish in my pain, wanting her to be here is a very hard thing for a Spirit to do so early in their passing because it takes a lot of energy from Spirit to manifest. I realised my longing for her was just to ease my pain, so I stopped asking for a while.

Mum kept sending signs though. Squirrels in the garden, we had seen many before her death; white feathers falling in front of me. A cool breeze on my face and whispers on the wind.

One night about three months after Mum passed, I saw myself walking down a cobbled street. I didn't recognize the street or the people around me. It was very warm and such a pretty place with cottages either side of the street. All of a sudden

I felt a hand touch my back. 'Hello, love.' I turned and there was my Mum. 'Lets go for a walk, love.'

I felt tears rolling down my cheeks. 'Mum! Are you okay?'

'Do I look okay?' came her reply. Oh yes she looked beautiful. 'Where are we?' I asked.

'It doesn't matter,' she said, 'just the fact that we are both here is all that matters.'

All of a sudden we were joined by my Grandparents. I felt so much happiness at being together again.

When I reached the corner of the street she had gone, saying 'Look after your Dad, love.'

'Of course,' I replied, not realising the true meaning of her words. When I woke up, I felt so strange, as if I couldn't connect with the earthly vibration for a while.

Rising Sun explained. 'When you dream of a loved one who has passed over, you are not dreaming they have come to visit you. Your conscious level drops and their vibration rises. That way they can connect more easily with you in your sleep state.' I felt so happy and privileged to be with Spirit in that way.

Everybody grieves in their own way, and it certainly doesn't help when you lose a loved one for people to say time heals. I don't believe it does, you just get on with life. One way of helping with this massive adjustment is to let off some balloons, each with their own personal message attached. The balloons fly free like your love for the departed person.

Rising Sun was so helpful at this time, coaxing me to keep working, helping me with the emotions I was feeling, and keeping me strong.

Around this time I came face to face with a possessed person, a first for me. A young girl came into the place where I worked and her Mother was with her. The girl was 19 years old, beautiful to look at, but there was an empty look about her. Her mother looked scared, tired and so sad. We went upstairs to my work room and the mother explained with much embarrassment that she believed her daughter was possessed. I reassured her that I would do all I was capable of doing.

The mother explained that it had taken four men to hold her daughter down at College when she had started to attack certain people, screaming and acting crazy. She said, 'This is not my daughter. She is a beautiful girl with a softness and gentleness, not a madness.'

All the time the girl just looked at me with no expression on her face. She said she would only talk to me if her mother left the room. I reassured her mother that we would be okay.

This was something new for me and once again I put my trust in Rising Sun. 'Be patient, Child,' (that word again) 'and not fearful because fear breeds fear.'

So I started the reading and the girl just kept staring at me. Suddenly she turned her head to the side and I felt the energy change. It was large and heavy and I couldn't get my breath for a moment. All of a sudden she spoke in a strange tone and with force. 'So you think you can help, do you? You who are nothing, you can't do anything for me. I have an angel on one shoulder and the devil on the other, and I know which one will win.'

I could feel my hands trembling and then felt Rising Sun's calm touch. I stood up and spoke, although I'm not sure who to.

'Now I really am not scared of you. You are the frightened one, after all why take over a gentle girl and try to destroy her? You will leave now and go to the light.' I felt the energy swirl around me.

'You have no place here anymore, and your jealousy and anger will no longer harm this girl. Go to the light, go to your own mother who is waiting to hold you and love you.'

I spoke louder. 'GO. LEAVE HER ALONE. THE ANGEL IS TRUE. THERE IS NO DEVIL. ONLY ANGER AND PAIN WITHIN YOURSELF, YOUR OWN SOUL. GO.'

I felt the energy diminish and watched the girl's colour return and a smile spread over her face. She seemed to relax and looked so beautiful. She then said, 'I feel so much better, alive again'.

We went downstairs to her mother who burst into tears. Two weeks later she rang me saying her daughter was back at College and was fine, thanking me so much.

Now I can't say for certain that this was some kind of evil possession that you see in the horror films, but what I do know is that I had felt and heard something that I didn't like. I had also felt the pain within this darker energy and watched the energy move into the light. I had listened yet again to my Guide, Rising Sun and put my total trust in him, and the result was a happy girl able to carry on with her life again.

The number of times I have heard those words! 'Patience, my Child. Patience.' I have wanted to scream back at times, 'Patience? I have none left.'

Funnily enough I always seem to find some, and have now become accustomed to waiting for the right time to do things and the right time for good things to come my way.

Being positive and seeing yourself in a happy place, inside and out, no matter how long it takes, will come sooner rather than later if you believe in the power of positive belief and cosmic support.

Nothing on the Spiritual level seems strange to me now. I realise that there is so much more to life than our day-to-day existence. I believe that we all have the ability within ourselves to create our own happiness and to make our dreams come true by positive thinking and picturing ourselves in a happy, healthy and abundant lifestyle.

About two months after my experience with the so-called possession, I felt another energy, lighter but powerful, with such warmth and love.

'Who are you?' I asked

'Archangel Uriel,' came the reply. 'I am your Archangel,' and such beauty lit up my room.

'You are so beautiful,' I said.

'Beauty comes from within, Child. This is my light shining. Please ask for what you need and I will do all I can to help you on your spiritual journey, for you are a teacher and a pupil. Please learn to accept my love and help, it is there for you.'

I thanked Uriel, feeling very guilty for not

believing in Angelic assistance. He read my thoughts and laughed out loud, 'You are not alone,' he said. 'Who else keeps picking you up, protecting you time after time? Do not fret, Child, you have no need to feel guilt or any other man-made emotion, only love.'

Angels are beautiful beings that walk the earth beside us day in and day out, helping us, laughing with us, crying with us, holding us, never deserting us, ever. My guardian Angel is called Saul. He is beautiful to look at with long blond hair and beautiful eyes that sparkle with light. He has a fun side to him that makes me smile when I am down, and he can talk to me whenever and wherever I am.

Now I totally believe that Angels can come to us as human beings during the worst moments of our lives. I have seen and heard of many occasions where a stranger approaches and helps you in your darkest hour and then disappears.

One such incident that comes to mind, although there have been many others, was just before Christmas 2014. My Dad is not a well man either physically or mentally, although he still keeps soldiering on. He is very stubborn, love him, and he decided to walk down to the shop which is about a quarter of a mile away, and walk back with shopping he didn't need. He is unsteady with a walking stick, let alone without!

I arrived at his house to find him gone, and was instantly worried, so I set off in the car to find him. I saw him walking with a boy of around 14 years old. I slammed on the brakes, and shot out of the car towards them. As I got closer, I could see the light shining from this boy. His hair was blond and wavy and his eyes were ice blue in colour. He handed me the bags and very calmly said, 'I was helping your Father carry these. He is a lovely man.'

He then smiled at me and he was beautiful, I thanked him and looked again, even his school blazer had the wings of an angel as a badge. And then he disappeared into the dusk.

Dad said, 'Funny. He just appeared from nowhere. That's twice that has happened.' He was an Angel, no doubt about it.

Life carried on as it does after the loss of a loved one and I soon realised that this was the start of another journey.

My Dad, who had always seemed so strong and capable, aged before our eyes. His heart had been broken by the loss of his dear wife, and he had a mental breakdown, although he tried not to let his children and grandchildren see.

He started to hoard things, things he didn't need. He would go shopping just so he could talk to people. He missed my Mum so much. Then he started getting pain in his chest on and off, not really telling us about it.

Things started to move forward rapidly seven or eight months after Mum's death. I moved into a lovely place in Winchcombe, renting the property with my partner at the time, only to split up with him a year later. I loved the house, it had so much character and the presence of a Spirit nurse who made herself known to me on the second night after we moved in. She was Victorian with long bustling skirts and high-necked dresses. She was always very busy, up and down the two flights of stairs, checking we were okay all the time. She had no desire to leave and I had no need to move her on. In fact I enjoyed her presence around me. I felt safe with her, even though she could be a bit brusque at times.

I was sad that my relationship ended. It didn't last long but I have no regrets as I learnt yet more valuable lessons. It was worrying when I noticed I was starting to build up a lot of debt due to only one wage coming in, which just about covered the rent and food.

So I started borrowing on credit cards. Never a sensible thing to do, but I loved the house and I loved Winchcombe, having lived there once before when I was married.

At work I was doing more and more readings and sat in on a Circle Group, developing and learning about every aspect of Mediumship and healing. I enjoyed dancing around my home and on summer nights had the back door open, loving the freedom and feeling of love from Spirit.

All the time the family and I kept an eye on Dad, who had now started to fall into a routine. I dreamt of family who had passed over and was so grateful in the knowledge that these weren't dreams but visitations from them. I started to like myself more and more, enjoying the way I looked after years of self-loathing, yo-yo anorexia and trying to be somebody different. I was now fitting in, not just in my own skin but in my own soul and Spirit too.

In 2005 my first grandson was born. It was a hot summer and as I watched my daughter bloom with pregnancy I knew this child was a boy. Emma decided that although she and David, a kind, loving man, were a couple, she did not want to move to Birmingham where David lived, so planned to move in with me once the baby was born.

He was two weeks late and eventually she started having contractions and we went to the hospital. I felt very honoured to be at the birth with her and David, but as things progressed I knew something wasn't right. After hours and hours of labour and an awful lot of blood, I knew Emma's waters had to be broken.

How do you tell a midwife something like that?

'I am a Medium and I am being told you need to break the waters.' I couldn't say it, so I started sending the message to her mentally. 'Please break her waters, please.'

After about five minutes the midwife said, 'I think I should break her waters.'

All of a sudden all hell broke loose. The baby was in trauma, doctors and nurses came and Emma was pushing like her life depended on it. In fact, the baby's life depended on it. He had swallowed his own faeces in distress and he came out lifeless. I watched him being born and kept reassuring Emma that he was okay. Suddenly he cried and they placed him in her arms, a beautiful angelic face, our little Angel Alfie had arrived and didn't we know it!

Right from the beginning Alfie would only settle if his heart centre was against yours. He screamed a lot and would arch his back. You could only settle him with a song or have him lying on you. My heart sank as I watched this little one fight the way I had done, and often when I came home after work, he would scream as he looked to the side of me. I had to ask the Guides to step away.

My daughter had years of no sleep, and both David and Emma despaired at times but loved him so much. I always slept in with him when he stayed at Winchcombe and his little body would relax against my heart centre. I so didn't want him to go through what I had as a child, but I could see exactly the same pattern evolving.

'Surely not?' I begged. 'Once is enough.'

But I asked to no avail, no answer. I knew then that this beautiful little boy was going to have a hard time of it.

As a family, we could not have been happier with his arrival and loved him dearly. I thanked Rising Sun for bestowing on him love and joy from the Angels and Spirit. I used to watch him grow calm as my son sang totally unsuitable rock songs to him and my heart would swell with love and pride. I watched as both my children grew spiritually with a knowledge beyond the living. I also thanked Spirit for their protection of both my children.

Emma lived with me for a few months, travelling

to Birmingham and David travelling to Winchcombe. Eventually she made the decision to move in with David and they would look for another house. The day she left broke my heart. I have always said, 'My soul was saved when each and every one of my grandchildren was born.' I cannot express the unconditional love I feel for each and every one of them. They are everything to me, and I felt so alone when Emma and Alfie went, but I knew she had to make her own life as a family with David.

From birth children are able to see and link with energy around people and every living thing. My advice both from Spirit and my own feeling, is to nurture and to watch how children respond to different things and to learn from them, as the innocence they are born with and the sheer delight they portray at seeing the aura and happy smiles of people is a sight to behold.

Even though I missed them dreadfully, I was able to meditate and enjoy my life in my rented house in Winchcombe, it was a sanctuary, protected from outside forces and loved so much. My work was still growing and I loved every moment of it, learning all the time, talking to Spirit and at times even asking them to please leave me alone so I could experience some peace and quiet.

Around this time my son met the girl who was to become his wife. He had known her at school, Victoria, a lovely quiet girl, and he was falling in love. All I have wanted for my children was their happiness and good health.

We were told by a revered Medium and Healer that their relationship wouldn't last, but I am pleased to say she was wrong, they are very happy.

Another lesson learnt: sometimes we as Mediums need to up our energy to hear all of the message we are being given in perfect detail, and not just half the message, as this lady had done.

Also around this time I met a man called Dave. Just over a year before our meeting, I was viewing a house with a friend for her to live in, when my attention was called by Spirit to look at the house opposite.

'I will meet the person who lives there and go out with him,' I announced to my surprised friend.

'He's abroad,' was her reply, 'he doesn't live here, just rents it out. So you won't be meeting him.'

'Yes I will,' I said.

About a year later, he walked into the place where I worked. He was dark and handsome and we talked and talked. He came to Winchcombe to see me and we started seeing each other. He moved in about five or six months later, 11 years younger than me, but it is good.

So began the next phase of my journey.

In 2007 Emma gave birth to another boy, our star Louie, a wise old soul who can never feel anything but love. Such a beautiful boy with a gentleness and an understanding of life that most people will never comprehend.

Again I thanked Spirit for his safe arrival. Louie is so different from Alfie, but right from the beginning you could see that Louie was the calm Alfie needed in his life. A beautiful happy little baby who shines so bright, his smile lights up a room. This time I was not at the birth, but sent my energy out to Emma to help her. I will talk about my other two grandchildren in my next book.

I soon realised that things were not as they should have been at work and that soon it would be closing down. I had learnt so much from the people I worked with, had expanded my reputation as a good Medium. I knew how to send lost souls to the light, how to connect to my guides, how to be proud of my gift and how to move forward in life.

What I didn't realise was that I still had a massive challenge to overcome, but for now I was feeling in a happy place. Approaching 50 I felt life was running forward. I still missed my Mum so much, but wanted to see the future unfold.

Suddenly I had a phone call. My Dad had had a heart attack and on further examination it was decided he needed a triple bypass. My heart sank once again. Please Spirit let him live. He will, they said, he will.

I raised my arms up to the sky and screamed in frustration and once again felt the arms of Spirit enfold me. I believe my Dad's heart had broken at the loss of his beloved wife Wendy, and now he needed all the love and healing I could give. I was not ready to loose my Dad, not now.

So began the next phase, which was to be so powerful and so difficult. For the moment I was allowed the blissful ignorance of not knowing, so that I could enjoy life and learn once again.